Tweet®
This!

How to Amplify
Your Brand on Twitter®

LAURIE
KRETCHMAR

Up With Social Media

Up With Social Media
San Mateo, CA

Ordering Information:
Quantity sales. Special discounts are available on quantity purchases by corporations, associations, and others. For details, contact the publisher at the email above.

Project Management: Marla Markman, www.MarlaMarkman.com
Book Design: Kelly Cleary, kellymaureencleary@gmail.com

Publisher's Cataloging-in-Publication data

Names: Kretchmar, Laurie, author.
Title: Tweet this! How to amplify your brand on Twitter / Laurie Kretchmar.
Description: Includes index. | San Mateo, CA: Up With Social Media, 2022.
Identifiers: LCCN: 2022909010 | ISBN: 979-8-9862068-0-6 (paperback) | 979-8-9862068-1-3 (ebook)
Subjects: LCSH Twitter. | Internet marketing. | Online social networks. | Branding (Marketing) | BISAC BUSINESS & ECONOMICS / Marketing / General | BUSINESS & ECONOMICS / Skills
Classification: LCC HF5415.1265 K74 2022 | DDC 658.8/72--dc23

979-8-9862068-0-6 (Softcover)
979-8-9862068-1-3 (eReaders)

TWITTER®, TWEET®, RETWEET® and the Twitter Bird logo are trademarks of Twitter Inc. or its affiliates.

This book is not affiliated with Twitter or any other products or services mentioned herein.

Printed in the United States of America

Contents

Advance Praise

"Have limited time to worry about social media? Read *Tweet This!* This savvy, concise guide shows busy execs what they need to know and how to amplify the brands, organizations and causes they're passionate about."

—Caroline Donahue, board member for GoDaddy,
   Experian, Emerge America, Computer History Museum;
   former CMO and EVP Sales, Intuit

"Entrepreneurs, consultants and high-fee experts need to offer value with their content, and this brilliant guide shows you how. If you've been waiting on the sidelines to maximize the power of Twitter, follow Laurie's advice straight to the bank. Do It!"

—David Newman, CSP, author of *Do It! Marketing* and
   Do It! Speaking

"Once you know your positioning, it's time to build your digital footprint. Laurie Kretchmar's guide will show you how to do just that on Twitter. I recommend it!"

—Andy Cunningham, president of Cunningham Collective
   and author of *Get to Aha! Discover Your Positioning DNA
   and Dominate Your Competition*

"For most consultants (and probably most business people) Twitter is the allspice of marketing—we know it's an important ingredient, but we're not sure exactly how to use it. Fortunately, this idea-packed little book completely demystifies Twitter. If you're running a business, you have to build visibility, and Laurie Kretchmar's book explains how to effectively add Twitter to your marketing mix. Highly recommended."

—David A. Fields, consulting firm advisor and author of
   The Irresistible Consultant's Guide to Winning Clients

"Laurie Kretchmar has created the unauthorized cheatsheet that us novices can use to master Twitter and connect with our clients' hearts about the things that matter to them."
—Petra Franklin, venture capitalist and artist

"I can't think of anyone better capable of explaining Twitter tactics to people seeking to build their personal brands. Laurie Kretchmar has counseled hundreds of professionals; you're in good hands."
—Stephanie Losee, global head of ABM and executive
   content at Autodesk and former head of content at Visa,
   Politico and Dell

"Laurie is an expert on Twitter, and this book is a must-read for professionals in tech, health care and other fields."
—Kristin Speer, executive recruiter

"Even if you've tweeted for many years, you'll find useful tips and reminders in this book. Plus, it's a great gift for your clients or manager."
—Christine Crandell, president of New Business Strategies and author

"I confess that I was a complete Twitter ignoramus. Reading this book helped me get up to speed. The book is like a gem—small but valuable."
—Robert W. Bly, copywriter

Intro:
A Note To Skeptics

Some might think it takes too long to learn Twitter or build a following.

To these folks, I say consider the tale of the French aristocrat who yearned to grow a certain tree. His gardener shook his head and said it would not reach maturity for decades.

The aristocrat responded, "In that case, there is no time to lose; plant it this afternoon."

That's the spirit. If you're serious about building your brand or writing that book, take steps to get launched on Twitter sooner rather than later.

How about now?

Glance at Chapter 3 for the Art of the Tweet.

Peruse the Glossary.

Happy tweeting. See you on Twitter!

—*Laurie*

@LKhere

Bonus Material:

Go to **upwithsocial.com/book** for even more tips, including a Twitter strategy worksheet, links to the tweets in this book, plus the latest information on Twitter's newest features.

1
Why Twitter?

Welcome! Thank you for picking up this book. I aim to teach you painless ways to amplify your brand, organization or favorite cause by using Twitter. We will even find a way to sneak in some fun stuff.

This book is for busy people whose main goal is building their businesses and living a good life, and as a result haven't had time to figure out all the nuances of Twitter. Or perhaps they started an account years ago, but it's been gathering dust ever since.

First things first. I'm a believer that once you have your overall business strategy in place and have a general idea of your positioning, it's time to build your brand. Think of the process as Create-Amplify-Build. First, **Create** your content strategy: Decide what makes sense for you, whether it's hosting webinars, writing scintillating blog posts and newsletters on a regular basis, crafting op-eds or a combination of the above. Then you need to actually generate the content—or hire someone to do it for you.

Next, you need to decide how you will distribute or promote your content to get it in front of those people who want to know about it. Or, in other words, **Amplify** it. That's the chief focus of this book.

Crucially, you'll also need to grow and cultivate your network. That's where **Build** comes in, another aspect we'll explore.

The result is more of however you define success: awareness by your target audience, publicity, thought leadership, reputation, people reached, a stronger brand, better connections.

If you have limited time (or, as we say in Silicon Valley, limited bandwidth) to spend on social media, this book is for you. I will fill you in on what you need to know and how to use Twitter to amplify the brands, organizations and causes you are passionate about. My focus is what PR people call "earned media" or free publicity, and "owned media," referring to your own website and blog.

First, let's tackle a few myths about Twitter:
Myth 1: You need a huge following to make an impact.
Nope. Just a few hundred people who are interested in what you have to say could be enough, if they're the right people. What if one of them was an editor at your industry's most respected publication, the head of the MacArthur Foundation "Genius Grant" committee or your next customer?
Myth 2: You need to be a young hipster who's fluent in memes.
No, thank goodness. That's TikTok (just joking).

Myth 3: You can just automate all your tweets.
Well, no. Just blasting out your own material with no interaction isn't the best strategy. In fact, this is the No. 1 mistake some people make. It's analogous to old-school broadcast media, as opposed to social media. Even Katie Couric and Dan Rather, stars from the broadcast TV era, interact with people on Twitter. So should you.

Now for three truths.
Truth 1: It's not a silver bullet for all your marketing.
Sadly, it's not. But is any one thing a silver bullet?
Truth 2: It will take some time.
So let's get started!
Truth 3: It might change a lot with a new owner.
Could be. All the more reason to dive in and see what the buzz is about.

Twitter, which hatched in 2006, has been described as a modern public square, a microblogging service and a publisher with massive reach and influence. Venture capitalist @SteveWestly calls it "the 21st century platform for CEOs" to communicate directly to their customers. In short, it should not be ignored if you're curious, interested in what's happening and want to make an impact.

Twitter has an estimated 436 million active Twitter users worldwide, and every day 229 million people and organizations use the platform. You, too, can find ways to build a presence and make it work for you.

Special bonus: Once you master Twitter—and that is an eminently achievable goal—you also will have taken a refresher course on using other social media. The principles are the same, and since social media platforms compete against and increasingly imitate one another, they end up with similar features. What works on Twitter will also help your posts on LinkedIn, Instagram and Facebook. If you follow my tips, you'll also become pithier and more community-minded as you build your brand and attain your overall marketing goals. There are many reasons to use Twitter.

My Top 3 Reasons

1) **Get in the game.**

Be a player. When a person (or brand) tweets, it provides an excellent snapshot of how they present themselves to the world. Prospective clients, podcast hosts, event planners, TV bookers and many other people can check a person's feed and get a quick glimpse of that person's offerings, wit and passions. In a phrase, it's social proof.

But if a person has no Twitter feed? That person isn't even in the game. Get in the game, especially if you're in marketing or sales. Or business or tech or science. In these industries—and indeed in almost any industry outside the clandestine—you want to present your best self to colleagues; Twitter is a brilliant and easy way to do that. You can start with baby steps by following people (more about that coming up). Get started now, because it's a slow pursuit with a future payoff.

2) **Amplify your interests and causes.**

   If you attend conferences, write blog posts, appear on podcasts, hold webinars, use audio apps, teach a class, publish a newsletter or even start to think about writing a book, you should invest some time in using Twitter. Period! Twitter is an ideal medium to "find your people" and share news with those who are most interested. At minimum, let others know when your events are occurring. After all, one of the most rewarding aspects of Twitter is that it helps you forge strong connections apart from the people who already know you—and get noticed for the right reasons.

   If your organization or company also has an official corporate account, you can amplify (share) your company's posts for wider reach, and, when appropriate, request that your company amplify yours (this cross-promotion is easiest when you own the company!). It's a win-win.

3) **Expand your horizons.**

   Discover what people are talking about. For starters, you can learn more about your customers and prospects by observing what they are saying. As Storyful, a social media newswire and news agency, notes, "Insights from social media can power marketing brainstorm sessions, allowing brands to create content marketing and advertising that consumers don't scroll past. Social media users are constantly sharing their perceptions, fears, challenges and frustrations. Contextualizing and analyzing these conversations enables brands to create content that speaks to consumer needs." In other words, paying attention to what your customers are saying can inform how you sell to them and what you say, too.

Twitter also gives you a glimpse into what's trending on other platforms. What are brands doing on TikTok? Which business celebs and other big names are pontificating on Clubhouse? Who is doing what on LinkedIn Live, Instagram Live or Twitch? You'll hear about it on Twitter.

You can also discover the delightfully unexpected. For example, the movie director Barry Jenkins (@BarryJenkins), not surprisingly, talks about movies. He's also developed a Twitter following among road warriors for his trenchant observations and videos while flying above the clouds on business.

Or take a look at the account of writer Trung T. Phan (@TrungTPhan). A prolific tweeter, he wrote a long thread on the insights he gained when he "went down a rabbit hole looking for cross-industry innovations," including how a pharma company borrowed innovations from a racing car pit crew to improve its production line.

So many people liked his thread of 12 tweets that it, as with many of his observations, was widely circulated. (To learn how to create and post a thread of multiple tweets, see "When you have a lot to say" in Chapter 3.)

Take a Break ☕

Need a break from work? Check out some of the major accounts known for humor, including @Wendys, the fast-food chain. (As they have tweeted, "We like our tweets the same way we like to make our hamburgers: better than anyone expects from a fast-food joint.") You may observe that Wendy's and other big brands sometimes aim for racy messages. Or see what your favorite authors or comedians are talking about. If you seek inspiration, humor or tips from other people, whether they're about parenting, mindfulness, travel or pets, you'll find plenty.

If you delve into the hot topic of podcasts to play on your next car ride, you may come across links to a viral podcast episode from *Reply All* about a song that stuck in someone's memory. "The Case of the Missing Hit," as it's called, is also a meandering tale about how the music industry has changed over the years.

Or try searching for museums worldwide that tweet about their collections. (Example: The Munch Museum in Oslo tweets as @munchmuseet.) Or search for people tweeting about art, NFTs, animals or science—whatever your interests may be. Or @HuffPoSpoilers to see short summaries of click-bait headlines.

More Reasons to Use Twitter

If the three reasons above are not enough to tempt you, here are five more reasons you should be on Twitter:

1) You'll gain a window into a younger mindset. As the noted Pew Research firm reports, Twitter users tend to be younger and have more education and higher incomes than U.S. adults overall. Marketers and people in tech and other fast-moving industries, take note!

2) Twitter can be a powerful way to communicate with people you haven't met yet and want to reach. Gefen Skolnick, the founder of Couplet Coffee, who goes by @chiefgayofficer, tweeted:

> "why is this founder always tweeting" because multiple investors I adore committed & wired via DM this week. that's why

Skolnick is a big believer in the idea that underrepresented people should establish a presence on Twitter to have a voice, level the playing field and reach customers, investors and other people who can help them with their business. (By DM, she means people sent her private messages on Twitter via Direct Message. More on that in Chapter 5.)

I know people who have landed a board seat or a job thanks to tweets—or, more specifically, conversations sparked on Twitter at just the right time. I personally landed a celebrity guest for a great cause when I saw on Twitter that she'd be in town the same week that my client was hosting a fundraising event. I reached out via DM, and she said yes.

3) Twitter is free to use, as are the other mainstream social media platforms. However, something to keep in mind is the wise saying that when a product is free, that means you, as the user, are not the customer but the product—served up to advertisers. This is something to keep in mind as you navigate this and other social media sites.

4) Learn and leverage new functionality. Twitter is working on ways to grow beyond ad revenue and is adding features, such as ways to monetize (make money from) your content. For example, at the top of some people's profiles, including that of contrarian investment advisor @Codie_Sanchez, you'll see a newsletter sign-up and a "subscribe" button. Typically there'll be a free version and then an option that costs a monthly fee.

The company has launched Twitter Spaces, social audio or audio rooms similar to the audio app Clubhouse, where you can listen or host conversations. You can try out these new features or wait to see which ones become most popular. (Tweet me at @LKhere or visit my website at **upwithsocial.com/book** if you have specific questions!)

5) You can benefit from Twitter even if you don't tweet! While I encourage people to tweet, especially if your goal is to amplify the impact of your business or

favorite cause, you'll still benefit from Twitter even if you just open an account and follow others. (My hope is that this book will inspire you to get off the sidelines and tweet a bit, too.)

TLDR for Doubters

- It's too hard: No! Actually, it's pretty easy. See Chapter 3.
- It's too time-consuming. It doesn't have to be. See Chapter 5.
- It's not effective (hmm). This book aims to convince you otherwise!

Overview: Who Needs Twitter?

If you're trying to build your brand and gain visibility, Twitter should not be missed. You'll find business owners, journalists, consultants, tech people, biologists and chemists, economists, real estate agents and opinionated venture capitalists. Not to mention news junkies, history lovers, parents, readers, Star Trek and space lovers, sports fans, dog lovers, cat people, hobbyists, and creators and fans of movies, TV, anime, livestreaming and other entertainment.

By having an account, you'll see for yourself how social media is a growth engine and an indicator of what's happening in the marketplace. Some 89 percent of consumers will buy from a brand they follow on social media, according to Sprout Social, a company that builds social media software for marketers. And 84 percent of them say they'll choose that brand over a competitor. Moreover, there's untapped potential: While marketers typically use social data to understand their audience, less than half use it to measure ROI or gain competitive insights.

If you've heard negative things about Twitter and are worried, that's understandable. However, many professional people find Twitter useful, and this book will show you how to use the platform to your benefit and avoid the pitfalls. Overall, I think the positives vastly outweigh the negatives and snarkiness. You can stay up to date on news of interest to you, make connections, share important info and—in the overused words of social media hype—be authentic. You can largely—if you want to—avoid the ugly side of Twitter.

Cheers to You

The fact that you're reading this book shows that you have an interest in learning more. That's great!

Since communities (like seeds, compound interest and other miracles) take time to grow, let's get started. But a word of warning: Twitter can be highly addictive! (We'll delve into ways to save time in Chapter 5.)

Need One More Reason?

If you're of the female persuasion, you're sorely needed on Twitter. Whenever you read about several professors or grad students doing interesting research, or you see a group of male and female professors on TV, you'll likely find that the men have active Twitter accounts. However, I frequently find that their female colleagues don't have accounts or haven't updated them in months due to lack of time or interest. (They may also have heard that Twitter can seem like a hostile environment to women.)

But if you want to build your brand, take a moment to tweet, especially when you have a professional accomplishment to share, such as a recent interview. If you know your book is getting reviewed, whether it's in *The New York Times* or your local hometown paper or your favorite website, prepare for your day in the sun by launching (or dusting off!) your account now.

I once reached out to a professor who hadn't tweeted in months and whose book had been glowingly featured that day in a major newspaper to say, hey, now's the perfect time to mention that book review! She thanked me and has been tweeting regularly ever since.

Keep in mind that certain people *want* to know your thoughts. If you're the head of HR at a tech company, prospective employees and new managers may be very interested in learning about the ins and outs of your company and your industry. Credit Karma's Chief People Officer Colleen McCreary, who tweets as @chiefpplofficer, posted a link to a podcast interview she gave, in which she compared herself not to the CEO of happiness but to a "product manager for the systems and tools that run the company." Very interesting insights for a job hunter or a fellow HR person.

And I love this sentiment, especially for shy people: Who are you *not* to share your ideas? Other people might find your insights impactful and useful.

Twitter is also the place to be if you hope to connect with people to invest in your company or if you plan to crowd-fund someday, either for a good cause or a business venture. So jump in and start building your network today—before you need the cash.

Before We Delve Further Into Twitter ...

Whenever I read memoirs or how-to tips, I like to know the writer's philosophy. Well, here's my Twitter philosophy: I find it endlessly fascinating. Twitter has a wealth of topical info shared by some interesting and thoughtful people. I like what some call "Nice Twitter." I avoid the unsavory stuff and the ill-informed. The people I follow include business leaders, teachers, professors, lawyers, scientists, astronauts, political candidates, TV writers, news junkies, recreational gardeners, authors, historians (some call themselves #twitterstorians) and others. I've met only a few of them in person, but I learn from them all nonetheless.

I interpret "business" broadly since just about all of us seek to earn money and reach the right customers. You'll find ex-amples in these pages from business and the tech industry, as well as eclectic examples from journalists, comedians, community builders, climate activists, a chef-author or two, the music industry and more.

My goal is for this guide to be highly skimmable. I hope you will zero in on whichever parts of this book are most crucial to you. For example, you could skim through Chapter 2 on how to get started, then dive into Chapter 3 (The Art of the Tweet) before going back to Chapter 2 to learn how to launch or update your account.

As you progress through this guide, you'll encounter the following:

Timeless Tips to help you get the most from Twitter

Tech Tips for the techier stuff

Fun Facts to share at parties

Peek at the **Glossary** whenever you need insight or a refresher on a term.

And feel free to check my website, **upwithsocial.com/book**, for bonus content and updates. Since Twitter, like other social media tools, continually tweaks their platform, the version you see may differ slightly from the version discussed in this book. For that reason, I focus mainly on concepts and content rather than technical details.

Stumped? To answer specific how-to questions, search for information at **help.twitter.com**

If by the end of this book I haven't persuaded you that Twitter is the place to be for building your brand and sharing your thoughts, and you'd still rather just watch the action and not comment (the term for this is "lurk"), I recommend you at least set up an account (to reserve your name if it's not already taken) and start following people and brands.

Now let's dive in and learn how to sign up in Chapter 2.

2
Where Do I Sign Up?

We talked in Chapter 1 about why businesspeople and professionals ought to try Twitter. Now, here's a quick overview on how to quickly set up an account and profile. In Chapter 3, you'll find more details on how to tweet and follow people, but for now let's get you up and running on Twitter, if you aren't already.

This book focuses on public accounts, where your posts are visible to everyone, since that's the easiest way to build your brand. (If you want to make your account private, visible only to select people, you can. However, you will restrict your visibility a great deal by doing this, which is at cross-purposes with building a brand, so I don't recommend it . . . unless you're a spy.)

The good news is that it's simple to create an account. But first let's talk about your username / handle.

Quick Take on Types of Accounts

1) **It makes sense to tweet as yourself.** If you only want to manage one account, I recommend doing it under your own name, as people find it more engaging to connect with a real person than a company.

   Some folks have accounts under their own names and their businesses. For example, venture capitalist Marc Andreessen tweets as @pmarca and has 962,000 followers, almost double the number of followers of his firm's account, which is @a16z.

2) **Personal vs. professional accounts.** You'll start with a personal account, which is a free account. Twitter now offers the option to switch, if you meet some basic criteria, to Twitter for Professionals. That type offers tools, some for no charge, for business, brands and creators, such as the ability to list store hours or accept monetary tips.

   If you decide to purchase ads to promote your tweets or gain followers, you'll need a professional account. You can switch then.

timeless tip

When you tweet at a corporate account, be polite! Remember that many people can see your remarks, and you don't want to be perceived as a cranky crank. Remember the Golden Rule.

Choosing Your Twitter Handle

If no one else is using it, select your own name. If your name is already taken, pick a variation (add a middle initial, use an underscore, use a nickname, etc.). You only get 15 characters for your username, aka handle, so if your last name is long you might have to truncate it. (Fortunately you also have 50 characters to display your real name, and even add some emojis if you wish.)

Some users (and teens) choose to hide their identities, but using your name will help build your brand.

Note that if you select a short nickname, such as Tex1, Twitter will automatically generate a unique string of numbers to distinguish it from similar accounts. Your name may end up as Tex157892, which looks like a bot or fake account and will scare off followers. If you have one of these names already, change it! For example, if you're a designer from Texas, you could swap that impersonal string of numbers for Tex_Designer or Tex_Designer1.

timeless tip — Choose your own name for the name you go by on Twitter, also known as your "handle," if it's available. It's a good rule of thumb for all social media.

With your desired name in mind, let's get going. While the details of the process may change over time, here are the general steps to take:

Step 1: Go to Twitter.com. Follow the prompts to "join Twitter." You may later wish to download the iOS or Android app so you can access Twitter on your phone.

For some of you, the prompts will be enough to get you going.

Start by signing up with your phone number or email address (or sign up with a Google or Apple ID).

Step 2: Now you'll be asked to provide

Your name (up to 50 characters)

Your phone number or email address

Your birthdate (to confirm that you're not a minor under 13).

Step 3: "Customize your experience." You can opt out by leaving this box unchecked if you don't want to see personalized ads or have Twitter "track where you see Twitter content across the web."

Step 4: You'll get a verification code via email or text.

Step 5: Set up a password. (If you aren't already using a password manager, I strongly recommend getting one for your security and sanity, and to track your passwords across devices. Popular password managers include Dashlane, LastPass and 1Password.)

Step 6: Choose your Twitter profile pic.

You can upload a good-quality headshot or other pic for a profile photo (or choose "skip for now"). There's a boring, rather nondescript image as a placeholder, which you can leave in place, although it will mark you as a newbie. A good photo is crucial for your credibility, although some people use whimsical images, such as a picture of a furry friend, a flower or a Memoji (an emoji likeness of themselves). Plan to upload your best recent casual headshot.

Step 7: Create a short bio.

You'll then be prompted to write a short bio. You won't have much room (just 160 characters). Twitter says: "Describe yourself. What makes you special? Don't think too hard, just have fun with it."

Again, feel free to choose "skip for now." As a person seeking to amplify your brand, this is an important step.

Read on for food for thought. You'll find a section and examples of a dozen dazzling Twitter bios.

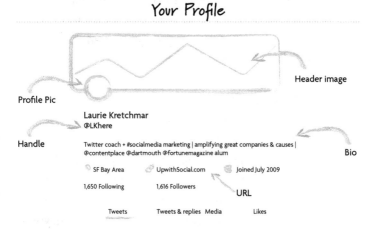

Your Profile

Header image

Profile Pic

Laurie Kretchmar
@LKhere

Handle

Twitter coach + #socialmedia marketing | amplifying great companies & causes | @contentplace @dartmouth @fortunemagazine alum

Bio

SF Bay Area   UpwithSocial.com   Joined July 2009

1,650 Following   1,616 Followers

URL

Tweets   Tweets & replies   Media   Likes

Step 8: Claim a username (you have 15 characters).

Step 9: Select your interests—a buffet of choices.

At this point, Twitter will ask you about your interests. You'll see multiple screens of topics for you to choose from to personalize your experience. The list goes on and on: business and finance, technology, sports, news, music, entertainment, lifestyle, arts and culture, government and politics, gaming, nonprofits, fun and science.

You'll also see lists of suggested prominent people to follow, such as the president and vice president of the United States, celebrities, and businesspeople like Elon Musk (@elonmusk) and ubiquitous marketing pundit Scott Galloway (@profgalloway). Keep an eye out for professionals in your field. You can choose just one and add more people later. You can also follow the people I've mentioned here to help you get started.

Voilà! You're almost ready to tweet!

Welcome Aboard!

You'll now be welcomed to Twitter. A few notes:

- There are other bells and whistles you can delve into later.
- In "More: Settings: Accessibility & Display," you'll find many options, colors and fonts to jazz up your main page. The primary issue to think about before you start typing is what *you* would like to communicate. Ask yourself: What makes sense for my personal brand?

- Overall, I highly recommend a profile photo, as mentioned. However, if you're just starting out on Twitter, you don't need to worry about a header image—yet!

When it comes to that big image at the top of your profile, a header image, remember that you have many options. For example:

- If you like a header image you're already using on Linked-In, you could use that one.
- If you have a book coming out, include visuals from your book.
- If you appear on a TV show or podcast, a related image could be your header. That's what former Reddit head Ellen K. Pao (@ekp) does—her current header image is a photo of herself talking with *Daily Show* host Trevor Noah.
- If you're not really sure what to post as a header image but love the beach or the mountains, feel free to use a favorite nature shot—your own or a copyright-free one.
- If you're promoting a specific product or service, you could, of course, use the brand or look. Microsoft's CEO @satyanadella currently has a collage of 24 photos of happy people working and learning. @ElonMusk has photographs of planets from space, including Earth.
- Do what makes sense for your brand. I highly recommend you look at what others are doing before you settle on something. And remember: It's easy to swap out your header photo and try something different.

In a hurry? **Jump Ahead to Chapter 3.**

You can change your Twitter handle at any time to a new name and keep your follower count, as long as the new name isn't already taken. Not many people know this, and it can be very powerful to rebrand later, if needed, with a higher base of followers.

fun fact

Bonus tip: Start a new account with the old name and post a placeholder tweet such as "Follow us at @_____ and list the new handle."

(**Short brag:** I helped a great cause amplify its brand by using this trick. They launched on day one of their new campaign with 3,000 followers instead of zero, which gave them excellent momentum and as a result were able to double their base within a few years.)

About That Bio

You can change your bio at any time (for instance, you could update it before you attend a conference by typing in "#Dreamforce2022"). Your bio is very "lightweight," as they say in tech circles, meaning it's easy to change. It's the opposite of carving a message in stone.

One way to let people know what you'll be tweeting about is to sprinkle your topics into your Twitter bio. (You could use hashtags, such as #innovation, for those topics.) If you initially skipped the step of writing your bio or want to update it, click on "Edit Profile" at the top right of your Twitter profile. You can also add a link to a website, whether it's a company website, blog or online store. It's a missed opportunity to leave it blank.

Sample Business Leader Bios

Here's a look at how some eclectic CEOs and business leaders describe themselves on Twitter, along with my thoughts. These are also people you may wish to follow for ideas and inspiration!

@Benioff

       ceo@salesforce.com chair@time.com

(*LK's Note:* Marc Benioff used to have a sentence in his bio that said, "All tweets are my own!" [As opposed to his PR team's or anyone else's.] However, as the CEO of a publicly held company, anything he says will, of course, reflect somewhat on his company, not just himself.)

@levie

       Lead Magician (and CEO) at Box (@box); Huge
       ABBA fan. I don't fully endorse anything I say
       below. Go [cloud emoji]

(*LK's Note:* Nice humorous touch about not fully endorsing his own tweets.)

@tim_cook [several emojis]

> Apple CEO Auburn Duke National Parks "Life's most persistent and urgent question is, 'What are you doing for others?'" - MLK. he/him

(*LK's Note:* He's mentioning several diverse interests, namely his alma mater, his love of national parks, and he has one inspiring quote and five emojis.)

@satyanadella

> Chairman and CEO of Microsoft Corporation

(*LK's Note:* Very straightforward, no frills, no emojis.)

@Indra_Noooyi

> Former Chairman and CEO of @pepsico. Profile photo by @annieleibovitz. My memoir, My Life in Full, is available now.

(*LK's Note:* Straightforward and showcases her book.)

@KatColeATL

> President & COO @athleticgreens, serving on boards, advising & investing in wellness/SMB tech/web3/CPG, life w/@daleyervin, ex COO & President @FOCUSBrands

(*LK's Note:* She's packed in quite a lot! Kat is telling us she's an expert in growing brands, and that she invests in wellness, small-medium businesses in tech, web3 and consumer packaged goods. She also mentions her husband and her former company, Focus Brands.)

@SallieKrawcheck
> CEO and co-founder @Ellevest. Past head of Merrill Lynch & Smith Barney, CFO of Citi, research analyst. Rabid UNC basketball fan. Author of Own It. Mom.

(*LK's Note:* Note the wide range of topics.)

Who Am I, in 160 Characters

For more inspiration about how people choose to describe themselves in their Twitter bios, here's a quick look at five interesting people and the succinct way they describe themselves. Again, these are people you may wish to "follow" on Twitter (to do so, just click the follow button).

1) Former Pandora corporate executive Joanna Bloor is now a leadership coach with a growing following for her flair in transforming people's personal branding from bland to memorable.
   > Here's the Twitter bio for @JoannaBloor:
   > I'm a Career #Futurist & #AmbitionGuide for the #FutureYou

2) Award-winning composer and actor Lin-Manuel Miranda (@Lin_Manuel), who used to tweet multiple times a day but then pared back, updates his bio

frequently. At one point it was this:

> he/him. Tweets going forward by Team LMM:
> Tweets by me signed "-LMM." Black lives matter.
> Now on Netflix: VIVO Upcoming: tick tick…Boom!,
> Encanto…

3) Here's the bio for astronaut Jessica Meir (@Astro_Jessica):

> NASA Astronaut. Comparative physiologist. Ex-
> plorer. Nature lover. Back on planet Earth after
> 205 days @Space_Station. Follow along on
> #TheJourney!

(*LK's Note*: See how she has used a hashtag for space enthusiasts.)

4) And here's a journalist:

> @laurenweberWSJ
> Workplace reporter @WSJ, author of In Cheap
> We Trust. RTs are not endorsements and likes are
> bookmarks.

(*LK's Note:* Lauren is saying that when she retweets (RTs) a tweet, she's not necessarily endorsing its content. She might just think it's noteworthy or of interest to others. Similarly, when she "likes" a tweet, she's using it as a reminder to herself to refer back to it as one would with a bookmark. As we'll discuss later in this chapter, however, retweets actually *are* seen as an endorsement of sorts, so be careful with them.)

5) Novelist @StephenKing, with 6.5 million followers, has a one-word bio:

>Author

I hope these examples spark some ideas for your Twitter bio. Come up with a brief way to describe yourself. Include a bit of your passions, whether it's cycling or being a self-described climate hawk. If you like, sprinkle in a few emojis. Don't sweat the bio too much; you can always refine it later.

Remember, your Twitter bio is very easy to change. If you attend a conference (or go to the International Space Station), you can add a hashtag temporarily to your bio to catch the interest of other conference-goers (or astronauts).

Wait Just a Second

If you want to take a break and refresh or update your big idea, positioning, value propositions, messaging, elevator pitches, and taglines, here are three good books: *Stand Out: How to Find Your Breakthrough Idea & Build a Following Around It* by Dorie Clark, *Get to Aha! Discover Your Positioning DNA and Dominate Your Competition* by Andy Cunningham, and *BrandingPays: The Five-Step System to Reinvent Your Personal Brand* by Karen Kang.

On Twitter, follow @dorieclark, @andycunningham4 and @karenkang.

Food for Thought

As you sign up for an account and think about your overall personal brand, including what you'll tweet about and when, ask yourself:

- What are my main areas of interest in using Twitter? (For example, marketing, startups, sustainability, cryptocurrency, companies in your region, women in business, leadership?)
- If I had to pick four or five topics to focus on, what would they be?
- Which thought leaders, celebrities, businesspeople, authors and others do I want to hear and learn from? Good news: I guarantee that you'll soon discover interesting people you didn't know existed.

Get ready for the "Art of the Tweet" in Chapter 3, where we'll talk about how to move from choosing your topics to actually tweeting and raising your profile.

3
The Art of the Tweet
(And Retweet)

And a Few Words About the Art of Spaces

B y this point, you've signed up for an account and penned a very short bio. In this chapter, we will discuss your first five tweets, cover the importance of photos and hashtags and talk a bit about video. Finally, we'll tackle the key questions of figuring out what messages and topics you'd like to talk about.

For starters, review the questions from Chapter 2:

Ask yourself:

- What are my main areas of interest in using Twitter?
- If I had to pick four or five topics to focus on, what would they be?
- Which thought leaders, celebrities, businesspeople, authors and others do I want to hear and learn from?

Your answers to these questions will inform the topics you tweet about. Fortunately, it's easy to update these topics as your interests change. In the meantime, search for information by searching for hashtags, which are phrases or words preceded by a hash sign, such as #innovation, #fintech,

#SaaS, #B2B or #Oscars2023. Hashtags make it easier for people to search for related topics. Hashtags are also used widely on Instagram, LinkedIn and other platforms.

fun fact Hashtags were invented not by Twitter but by an active user!

Anatomy of a Good Tweet

What makes a good tweet? It sounds like a philosophical question that could be debated at length, but you have a great deal of latitude. A tweet is simply a message that can include text, links, images and video. Here are some essential tips:

- It's OK to just have text. In fact, that's how Twitter started.
- However, you'll attract more interest if you add an image or video to your post.
- Use accurate Twitter handles (don't just guess at a person's handle, as you may be wrong). If you use the incorrect handle, the sky won't fall. However, you'll lose impact—the person mentioned may never see it and it will look like a broken link.

Here's a simple, straightforward tweet from sales strategist Colleen Francis (@EngageColleen):

Anatomy of a Tweet

Colleen Francis
@EngageColleen

There are three universal truths about selling to people.

280 max. characters

Find out what they are here: http://ow.ly/35Cz50H8ocN

#SalesGrowth #SalesTeam #SalesLeadership

Blog Link

Hashtags

KNOW
THE
RULES

Image

Reply   Retweet   Like   Share
              Quote Tweet

Colleen Francis shared the headline of a blog post on her website (she tweeted, by the way, several months after the post went up, a good example of getting continued mileage from your content). She included hashtags for others interested in the perennial topics of sales growth, teams and leadership.

How to Find Twitter Handles

Make sure when you refer to other people or companies in your tweets that their Twitter handle is accurate. Double-check a person's handle—it's not always their name, and the actual handle might not be what you'd expect. For example, two of Twitter's co-founders use only their first names: @jack and @ev. *The Washington Post* media columnist

Margaret Sullivan goes by @sulliview, while Cheryl Contee, author and investor in innovative startups led by women and women of color, goes by @ch3ryl.

Your First 5 Tweets

Remember that you have many possibilities. Here are some ideas.

1) Say hi. In your own words, say how glad you are to be on Twitter.
2) Look around for a tweet from someone else that you think is interesting. Retweet it by clicking the retweet button underneath the text. (That's the one that looks like a continuous arrow.)
3) Look for another tweet from a brand you trust, and click the retweet button. Now select "quote tweet." Add your two cents along with the retweet, such as "Excellent insights" or, if it's humorous, "Funny."
4) Link to something online you would like to amplify, such as a blog post. Just as when you're crafting a subject line for a newsletter or a juicy headline for a blog post, think of some catchy words to inspire others to read it. (Unless you're a big-name author, don't just type, "Something I wrote.") Include the link.
5) Repeat #4. Add some relevant hashtags, such as #sustainability or #quotes.

Congrats. You've just sent out your first five tweets. (And take your time—you don't have to do all five in one afternoon.)

Not sure of a handle? Here are two ways to find them:

On Google, search for their name in quotation marks and then the word Twitter, like this: "Cheryl Contee" twitter. Boom! You'll find their handle nine times out of 10.

Or on Twitter, type their name, click on the People tab and skim to see if they're listed.

Follow

I highly recommend you follow some of the people I've mentioned earlier in this book, even if you're not into musical theater or the aeronautics industry. See what they're tweeting about and if it appeals to you then follow—if it doesn't, you can always unfollow (just click the "Following" button at the top right of the person's homepage and select "Unfollow"). Speaking of people to follow, please follow me. Go to twitter.com/LKhere, click "Follow" and say hi! I aim to tweet back. You may also want to follow:

@Twitter Support for help and announcements
@TwitterMktg and @TwitterBusiness for tips on ads

You might wonder if following people who can't immediately help you build your brand will "clutter" your newsfeed. If you're just starting out, don't worry about that. For now, focus on observing what others do. Also, for a savvy way to follow many accounts, learn about the feature known as Lists (Chapter 5)!

Listen

"Listen" used to be a metaphorical term on social media, meaning to peruse what people are saying and pay attention to what they're talking about. But now that Twitter has launched Spaces (similar to Clubhouse, the audio app), you can literally listen to people having discussions. For more on Spaces, see the end of Chapter 3. (To find Spaces, look for purple circles at the top of your Twitter feed, representing audio conversations underway by people you follow. If no purple circles are visible, search on the Spaces icon, a microphone, to find other conversations.)

The main concept, whether with regular Twitter and Twitter Spaces, is to observe. Pretend you're Margaret Mead observing humans or Jane Goodall studying chimps. What are people talking about? If you read a person's bio, is it of interest to you? Does a tweet seem insightful and clever to you? Consider following them. Inane and not worth your time? Unfollow. Also see how people are responding to others' tweets.

Twitter Spaces

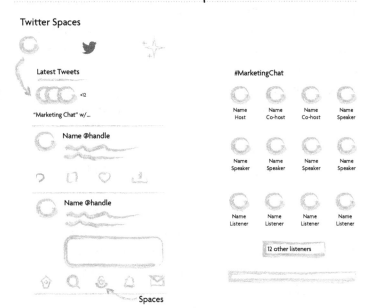

Photos and Videos Rule

We've all heard that age-old saying, "A picture is worth a thousand words," and it's definitely true for social media. Studies show that you will draw far more interest and engage more people if you use images. And video clips attract even more attention. (We'll get into the ins and outs of photos and videos later in the chapter. Let's focus on what to tweet about first.)

Topics to Tweet About

What's on your mind, workwise? What tips, insights and news do you want to share? What works best for your brand?

As you saw from the sample Twitter bios in Chapter 2, there's room to be serious, but also for wit and humor.

Here's a memorable tweet from the outspoken CEO Aaron Levie (@Levie) after his tech company Box went public in 2015:

> To those wondering what my tweets would be like after going public, all I have to say is [REDACTED]!

Some new Twitter users wonder what they could possibly say that others will find interesting. The short answer is: Lots! Remember the key topics and hashtags that you thought about while writing your Twitter bio. What do you want to be known for?

Certain topics such as human resources, leadership, start-ups and marketing can be of widespread interest, particularly when you provide insights, lessons learned, mistakes and your biggest challenges.

When I'm looking for possible tweets, I keep an eye out for insights about leadership and management, particularly having to do with women in business. Here's a tweet I mentioned in Chapter 1: Credit Karma's Colleen McCreary was interviewed by a venture capital firm about her innovative approach to being a chief people officer. It caught my eye, and I tweeted the following:

Refreshing idea for Chief #People Officer: Not chief of yr happiness, not CEO of culture. "I am like the product manager of the systems & tools that run the company"
- @Chiefpplofficer Colleen McCreary @creditkarma @Intuit. Via @firstround
https://review.firstround.com/the-chief-people-officer-as-pm:-rethinking-the-systems-and-tools-that-run-the-company... #PM #womeninbiz

(In the above I tagged her companies, Intuit and Credit Karma and the VC firm First Round, so they would see it and perhaps retweet it, and I added two hashtags: #PM for product management and #womeninbiz.)

For me, sharing interesting news serves several purposes: I hope it's useful for other people, shows my "nose for news" and helps me cultivate good relationships. And my tweets are an ongoing resource where I can easily scroll back or do a quick search to find something noteworthy.

To provide extra value and improve the odds that someone else will share my tweet, I tag relevant people. Let's say I'm tweeting about an interesting interview with a businessperson. I'll make sure to include the Twitter handles of the interview subject and the writer, which will automatically link to their profile pages and notify them about my tweet. That way they'll see it—and perhaps they'll retweet it, too.

The good news is there's no one right way to tweet. As in

life, there are many approaches. Here are a few styles:

On all day: Journalist Kara Swisher (@karaswisher) tweets many times throughout the day. If you were an upcoming guest on one of her podcasts or a PR person pitching a story, she would give you a ton to consider about what's on her mind and her views. Guy Kawasaki (@GuyKawasaki), former Apple evangelist and startup expert, is open about how he pays a team to tweet and post constantly on his behalf. I don't recommend this all-consuming method.

Witty observations about tech life: These can be insightful and entertaining. See @anothercohen. Also @yayalexisgay.

Snarky, snide, sometimes fun: Many do this, too. Not my style to be snarky, especially for business. It can be fun, though, as a break from work to see what comedians are saying. See @stevemartintogo. It could spark an idea!

Tweetable tips: Many people post these on a regular cadence, including salespeople, startup entrepreneurs and marketers. I like to share good ones when I hear them, such as this insight from a podcast when the host interviewed psychology professor and expert on influence Robert Cialdini. I retweeted the podcast link and added this comment:

Pro tip: Ask for advice to inspire customers to feel like co-creators in your product or service's success. Asking for feedback or opinions doesn't have the same effect, per @RobertCialdini in this convo w/ @LewisHowes.

New stuff: It can be fun to gain a glimpse of new products not yet on the market. Jane Manchun Wong (@wongmjane) has earned a loyal following for her insights and detective work about upcoming Twitter features.

Quotable quotes: A man named Jon Winokur (@Adviceto Writers) tweets excellent quotes about writing, such as this one on fiction (he has a huge following, by the way):

Names are very important because a lot of atmosphere comes with a name.
IRIS MURDOCH

fun fact

On any public Twitter profile, click on "Media" to see the tweets that the account has published with images or videos. It's a fun, sometimes useful way to observe what others are doing and gain ideas and insights.

Suggestions for Tweets

As for actual content, here are some ideas to inspire you. Note that there are always many possibilities. Which ones work best for you and your brand?

- **Humblebrag:** In these posts, you brag about a good deed, whether it's a team activity, a charitable event or both. Suppose your work team volunteered at a food bank, such as Second Harvest of Silicon Valley. A tweet like this one (along with a photo) could inspire others and prompt a return tweet from the food bank:

  > Our team at [company] was glad to lend a hand at @2ndHarvest.

- **Coming soon:** This is a giant topic ripe with many possibilities. Think about what's on your calendar and which events might be of interest to your prospects and peers. What's coming up in the next 6 to 12 months? Are you headed to an interesting conference? Being interviewed on a podcast? Going on a business trip? Looking forward to an awards show, a sporting event, a holiday or an election? All can be good fodder for your observations on Twitter. Search for a related hashtag, use it and you're likely to find others interested in the topic as well. Organized people will want to make an editorial calendar so they can track and schedule these topics in advance.

- **You're invited:** If you seek to attract people to a webinar, an in-person event, a store opening, a conference or a volunteer opportunity, you'll need appealing ways to catch their attention.

- Here's an example of an engaging tweet by a passionate person tied to a specific event:

> @NicoSGonzalez
> Starting tomorrow and running through January 5, tens of thousands of amazing humans will count birds all across the Western Hemisphere. It's a winter tradition 120 years in the making, and I love each and every champion who participates. https://audubon.org/news/the-key-christmas-bird-counts-120-years-success-people

Nico went on in other tweets to talk about how volunteers could still sign up to participate. He works in communications for the @AudubonSociety, "the original tweeters."

I had never heard of this annual bird-counting phenomenon before, but his tweet was a smart way to spread the message and find more bird-loving volunteers. It also gives you a glimpse of who he is as a person and is far more appealing than a dry request for volunteers.

timeless tip

Create an editorial calendar—a list of upcoming events and holidays—and use it as a tip sheet of possible topics to tweet about.

When you're in the news: Tweet whenever you're in the news or making news. If you write an op-ed or blog post or are quoted in an article, be sure to tweet about it.

- **Podcast appearances:** If you are interviewed on a podcast, you can not only tweet a link to the podcast, but you can also create a video clip (even if the podcast is audio only!) to accompany it. Audiogram is a cool tool that lets you select a quotable quote and then shows the words and sound waves on-screen. My tech team has created these for clients as diverse as Atma Connect (@AtmaConnect,) a nonprofit creating "tech for good," and ViridisChem (@ViridisChem), a biotech company that provides a chemical toxicity tool for scientists.

- **Same piece, many headlines:** The major news websites, including *The New York Times*, CNN and TechCrunch, come up with multiple ways to tweet about the same article or package; you can do the same. Vary the headline; vary the hashtags; and, if you have them, you can also vary the images. Indeed, in the podcast example above, you could easily select two different sound bites for two attention-getting tweets.

- **Interesting tidbits:** When you come across a thought-provoking article or some groundbreaking research, tweet a quote and a link and be sure to add a hashtag. Wharton School (@Wharton) professor Ethan Mollick (@emollick), who studies innovation, entrepreneurship and, as he says, "ephemera," routinely tweets highlights from research he comes across.

- **Mine hashtags for material:** Suppose your focus is #B2B—businesses that sell to other businesses. Search this hashtag and you'll find tons of tips and links to blog posts, podcasts, videos, case studies, white papers and technology. All this is a rich vein that you can mine for content for your tweets.

> ∞
> **timeless tip**
>
> Retweet, don't just like! Retweets are good karma; they reach more people than likes.

good karma
retweet! don't just like

The 80/20 Rule on Twitter and in Life

Have you heard of Vilfredo Pareto, the Italian economist who first came up with the 80/20 Rule (later named the Pareto Principle) during the early 20th century? The idea is that 80 percent of results often come from 20 percent of a cause or action. For example, 80 percent of a company's sales might come from 20 percent of its customers—or 20 percent of the sales team.

The 80/20 Rule is a useful guideline for tweeting, too. Aim to have 80 percent of your tweets supporting others or talking about topics of interest to people in your network. The remaining 20 percent can focus on your business and its offerings.

Other experts say to aim for a 3:1 ratio, or 75 percent to 25 percent. Regardless of the exact split, I hope you get the idea—most of your tweets should not be about promoting your company. You'd put people to sleep.

fun fact

When are people most likely to share their thoughts on social media? Personal milestones, sporting events, natural disasters, holidays, political events, pop culture moments and award shows. Source: Sprout Social

Twitter Counsel for a Small Marketing Team

The following are insights I shared with a B2B company that wanted to know what to tweet about and how often. These tips are also relevant for businesses that sell to consumers.

1) **How often should you tweet?**

Since there are only so many hours in a day, you must

approach Twitter strategically. Here's a basic plan I recommend:

- Create an overall editorial calendar of the best content you have and know about in advance: blog posts, webinars, new customer stories, conferences and major holidays, such as the Fourth of July, Thanksgiving, Christmas, Hanukkah and Kwanzaa.

- Sprinkle in partner content. Don't have any obvious partners or allies? Brainstorm who would be a natural fit. What associations or alumni clubs do you belong to that would be happy to amplify your message—since it dovetails with their main messages—to reach more people?

- On slow days, promote clients' tweets "opportunistically"—when industry media have positive news coverage about them. When that occurs, tag the writer's name (by including their Twitter handle), the publication and your client so the tweet gets maximum exposure. If you only include one of these, it's less likely to get noticed.

- When you have time, "like" positive and witty tweets by end users (in B2B, that's the customers of your customers) from the corporate account. (For an added bonus, your sales reps can go to your company's Twitter profile and see them tagged under the "like" tab.) If the comments are terrific—with high praise for your company—do a "quote tweet," where you share the original tweet and add a comment, which could be as simple as "Glad to hear."

For example, suppose one of your clients is the mall pretzel vendor @AuntieAnnes. If someone posts something positive like the following from Jay Scott (@LemonadeJay), retweet it! It's good karma:

> In just a couple short days my Bake-At-Home @AuntieAnnes Pretzel Kits will arrive. I can smell them cooking now.

2) **How can you make your company's content stand out?** For maximum visibility, pin the most important tweet (such as an upcoming webinar) to the top of your Twitter profile by clicking on the three horizontal buttons at the top right corner of each tweet and choosing "Pin to your profile" from the drop-down menu. (A pinned tweet must be your own; it won't work if you try to pin someone else's post to your profile, even if it's one you retweeted. You can also pin favorite content on your LinkedIn profile or Facebook company page). You can only pin one thing at a time, but you can easily change your pinned content at any time.

As noted earlier, it's smart to reuse and share your content multiple times. Media sites, including CNN, *USA Today*, Buzzfeed and the *Harvard Business Review*, repeatedly tweet about their top 20 or so stories throughout the day. Just make sure to vary the wording.

Also seek out allies—people with shared interests who will promote your content. Many nonprofits and cause-related membership organizations excel in this area. Look around for good examples, such as angel investor network New Media Ventures (@NewMediaVenture) and organizations that support your favorite cause. (For more on this strategy, see Chapter 4.)

3) **What's a framework for how to write a tweet?**

The following post from Drift, a sales enablement company, is a good example. Here's how @Drift promoted a success story in an interesting way, starting with a quote from a corporate client called Keet Health:

> "There's never been a better time to put customer-centricity into action. We knew we had to help our customers and community-at-large." Learn how @KeetHealth used Drift (finger pointing downward emoji) to onboard 35 new clients in 40 days during the COVID-19 outbreak. drift.com/blog/keet-health-success-story

This tweet has the following strong points:
- a catchy quote to pull the reader/prospect into the customer's story
- an appealing photo of the customer company (a type of photo that could serve as a template for other

examples of customer success stories)
- an emoji, which, used sparingly, can be fun
- a link to Drift's company blog

To make Drift's post even better, I'd add anywhere from one to four relevant hashtags (perhaps #customers, #CX for customer experience, and #health), plus a small version of Drift's logo on the photo. Also, go for the biggest bang: Always let the client know the article/blog post/social media post is going up and suggest they share it on their channels to make an even bigger splash.

Be sure to use hashtags that are relevant to prospective customers (such as #leadership or #Dreamforce22 if you're going to a certain tech conference).

In summary, as a general guideline, approach social media the way you would any marketing campaign, blog post or ad: Create and promote good content, messaging and stories in service to your overall goals. Then adjust as needed.

timeless tip Double-check a person's handle. It might not be what you think it is.

Make New Friends

The Girl Scouts sing a song inspired by an old poet with timeless wisdom: "Make new friends, but keep the old." Similarly, take a minute to think of Dale Carnegie's famous self-help book, *How to Win Friends and Influence People*. He advised talking "in terms of the other person's interest." As he said in his book, first published in 1936 and still relevant in the 21st century, "Remember that a person's name is, to that person, the sweetest and most important sound in any language." (OK, not everyone loves their own name, but you get the idea. Use people's names and Twitter handles.)

You must have friends and allies (your people, your tribe, your community) to amplify your messages. Make friends and ask them (strategically) to share. If I'm a customer and agree to be featured in a case study, interview or blog post, why wouldn't I promote the material? It would be mutually beneficial, a win-win.

I've had excellent success tagging business schools, universities and industry publications in relevant posts. Their social media manager or team will likely see your tweet, and there's a good chance they'll retweet it, thereby reaching a wider audience.

Organic Boosts

Similarly, if you cite/mention/tag an author or publication with an active Twitter account, they are likely to retweet your message, which will reach many more interested people organically, without you having to pay for an ad.

I followed this principle when tweeting for an executive coach who had written a leadership essay in which she cited an interesting study. We looked up the handle for the study's author, and our tweet was retweeted by @APA_Journals, with more than 21,000 followers, increasing the potential audience size for the essay and raising her profile among her target clients.

As the saying goes, rinse and repeat. Try these tactics out for yourself, track the results and see which social media posts get the most engagement and impressions. Then tweak your strategy accordingly.

A Word About Endorsements/Retweets

Let's face it: A retweet is an implicit endorsement. By choosing to retweet something, you are implying it's worthy of interest. A journalist or activist might retweet something they find horrific, scandalous or objectionable, but in business, I strongly recommend erring on the side of only sharing content you like and respect. If you want to comment on a sketchy issue, do so as a reply or comment on the original post; don't retweet the offending material yourself. (In fact, some people will take a screenshot of the offensive post to avoid giving it extra clicks and then post their comment about the screenshot.) What you don't want is for people to get the mistaken impression that the offensive message was yours, particularly if you oppose it.

How to Respond to Attacks

What should you do if you face criticism or abuse on Twitter?

In general, don't waste your time on Twitter fights. Here are ways to cope:

- If it's a legitimate criticism or comment, respond once or more to acknowledge it.
- If it's someone who seems like they're on a vendetta or missing the point, try not to engage.
- If necessary, mute them so you don't see their tweets or block them so they can't see your tweets.
- If they're abusive, report them: go to help.twitter.com

For more on the topics of fighting online abuse and tightening digital safety, search on the internet for @PENAmerica's Online Harassment Field Manual. You'll find tools and resources including guidelines to protect your online presence, strategies on how to respond to online abuse and advice on how to practice self-care. Also search on Twitter for the hashtag #FightOnlineAbuseNow.

When You Have a Lot to Say

When there's a lot on your mind, you may wish to post a series of tweets, which is known as a thread. There are some tech investors and startup founders who do this quite a bit, such as tech investor Codie Sanchez (@codie_sanchez). Author and political observer Teri Kanefield (@Teri_Kanefield) is another example of someone who uses threads and has gained a big following.

A visually interesting way to capture people's attention is to share information in a long thread, leaving lots of white space in between each point and adding emojis. As more than one tech person has noted, it can take up a lot of space and attract attention.

There are two main ways to create a thread:

1) You can reply to your own tweet just as anyone else would. However, if other people start responding in between your replies, it can get confusing for others to follow your thread later because it will be broken apart with gaps instead of being one continuous narrative. (One solution is to try numbering each individual post in your thread.)

2) Or, better yet, use the native Twitter thread tool built into the platform. Start a tweet and you'll see a small plus sign (+) under the message field. Create each of the tweets. Then click "tweet all."

   Sometimes you'll see followers of a thread tweet "@threadreaderapp unroll." Then a third-party app replies with a link to all the tweets on a web page in one easy-to-read format. Be aware that some users don't like this practice, as it diverts people to another site to see the conversation. People could just stay on Twitter and follow the thread.

tech tip

If you begin your tweet with a Twitter handle, it will only be seen by the people who follow both you *and* the person you're addressing in the tweet. If you want it to be visible to everyone, then put either a space or a period (.) in front of the handle.

For example, this tweet will only be visible to those who follow both the CEO of Twitter *and* my account:

> @paraga When will there be a Twitter edit button?

But this tweet, with that added period at the beginning, will go into my feed and be seen by all my followers*:

> .@paraga When will there be a Twitter edit button?

*Full disclosure: A tweet being "seen by all my followers" is a misnomer. All your followers will never be online at the same time to see any one tweet. However, it's an easy round number by which to calculate Twitter audience size.

Let's Talk About Visuals

Now that you have some good ideas regarding what to tweet about, let's talk visuals. Again, there are many possibilities. If you have a savvy marketing team, congrats—this will be easy for you. If you're a solopreneur, you could use your own photos, create your own graphics with Canva or Photoshop, hire a graphic designer or a friend with design skills, subscribe to a high-quality photo website (like Getty Images) or look for free photo and image sites (such as Unsplash, Pixabay and others). Or do a combination of the above!

Hello? Will people see your image?

Will it show up in their feeds?

Check before you tweet to discover whether an image will display in your followers' Twitter feeds or be hidden from view and appear as text-only, which garners less interest. Go to Twitter's Card Validator and type in the URL of the image you would like to use for a sneak peek of how it will display:

tech tip

https://cards-dev.twitter.com/validator

If it doesn't display, you can work around it by clicking on the photo button and uploading a photo from your desktop instead.

> **tech tip**
>
> Check out Sprout Social's list of 37 free image creation tools:
> https://sproutsocial.com/insights/free-image-creation-tools/

What Size for Your Images?

Social media platforms and sites display images at different sizes; it's definitely not one-size-fits-all. When you create that perfect tweet and the image to go with it, you'll want to optimize the image for each platform you use it on (or at least for your favorite platform) so it looks decent. You don't want to end up with a close-up of an elephant's side instead of an entire elephant.

The best resource to double-check the correct sizing for photos and videos on social media platforms (including Twitter) is the aptly named Sprout Social Always Up-to-Date Guide to Social Media Image Sizes. Find it here: https://sproutsocial.com/insights/social-media-image-sizes-guide/

Video Is the Bomb

Video is taking over the world. Some 86 percent of businesses use video as a marketing tool, according to Hubspot, the marketing software company, and 93 percent of marketers who use video say that it's an important part of their marketing strategy.

Movie studios and sports shows know they'll reach many

fans and prospective fans with punchy clips. In fact, video does more than raise awareness; it also can increase conversion rates by 65 percent, according to Hubspot. (Conversions could be anything from a prospective customer filling out a form to making a purchase, depending on your site's business goals.)

On Twitter, video clips that are 60 seconds or shorter will automatically loop. So when Michael (@kretchmar), a marketing guy, shows off his chocolate lab romping at the beach on a snowy day, the seven-second video continues playing until you stop it.

It's easy to upload video clips from your phone, just as you would with a photo. Select the clip, and click or tap on the image at the bottom of the tweet. Done.

Take a moment to be inclusive, and type in alternate text for viewers with impaired sight. (This should describe the contents of the video or photo briefly for those people who cannot view it.)

Twitter Spaces, aka Social Audio

During the COVID-19 pandemic, a new app called Clubhouse launched in the U.S. in 2020 and quickly gained a large following for "social audio," which is like listening to talk radio. Twitter provides space for these types of conversations, dubbed Twitter Spaces. If live audio conversations are of interest to you, follow @TwitterSpaces. Learn how to create or schedule a Space, host a ticketed Space in which you set ticket prices and audience size, and more.

What's the main benefit of hosting a live event? For music publicist and programmer Deb Hill (@debsYjhill), who was a beta user for Twitter Spaces, it's a way to meet many people and build her networks. She now knows many creators who aim to sell tickets to events, among other moneymaking opportunities. She listens to certain conversations much as she might listen to music—in the background while she's running errands or cooking.

To find Spaces, look for purple circles at the top of your Twitter feed, which show Spaces happening now hosted by people you follow. On a mobile app, look for the microphone icon. Follow @TwitterSpaces for the latest updates.

Explore and a Moment for Moments

Twitter Moments are collections of tweets about a single topic or event that create a slideshow effect. (At my Twitter profile you can see one I made about the lustrous, beautiful illustrations of the late artist Trina Schart Hyman, who was one of the most interesting people I've ever met. I wanted to draw attention to this talented artist and showcase my interview with her.)

To create a Moment, log in to twitter.com, and in the menu on the left-hand side select "More" (three parallel dots) and then "Moments." Note, however, that this is an older feature that Twitter seems to be de-prioritizing.

Click on Explore (the pound or hashtag sign) to find

trending topics, topics "for you" and more.

Next, we'll explore how to find people who share similar interests, such as #cybersecurity, #fintech or #twitterstorian (for history buffs).

Control who can reply, for example, on controversial topics: When you craft a message you'll see an option to designate who can reply: everyone, people you follow or people you mention.

4
Find Your Communities

You've launched your Twitter account, and you have some ideas for topics to tweet about. Now let's dive into how to find "influencers," people with similar interests and sizable followings, and journalists and podcasters covering your areas of interest. In short, how do you find your squad (or team of supporters), build your audience and find the people you'd like to reach?

Good question. It can be tricky and take time, so I'm glad we're talking about it now.

The ideal situation for forging connections is when you can meet a person in real life, such as at a meeting, conference or convention, and also online via their social media. It's not always possible, but it can be powerful when it happens. Twitter, by itself, is not a communications silver bullet. However, it can be a handy tool to help you get to know people's thoughts and help them learn more about you.

Sometimes you'll encounter someone on Twitter first and then arrange to meet up in real life. That's how Amy-Willard Cross (@amy2pt0), founder of the company and rating system GenderFair, met author, diversity expert and public speaker Minda Harts (@mindaharts). First, they met on

Twitter, then they connected in person in New York. CEO, author and passionate connector Susan Spector McPherson (@susanmcp1) has met people on Twitter whose weddings she later attended!

It's a win-win when you find people who are happy to promote your post because it matches their interests. For example, someone who wants more people to understand the urgency of businesses adapting to climate change might be very willing to share your tweets on the topic.

6 Ways to Find People of Interest

Try these methods to find people you'd like to know more about, such as a thought leader or a prospective client. Ideally, some of these people will want to follow you back.

1) *Search on Twitter.* Search for hashtags or subjects of interest. There's a terrific advanced search function shown starting on page 64. Find it at
   https://twitter.com/search-advanced

2) *Glance at the trending hashtags and "What's Happening."* These are topics that are currently popular on Twitter. You don't want to spend too much time here, but it's worth a look.

3) *Mine conferences.* There's gold in an event's speaker and attendee lists. Who else is attending? Look up a few of those people on LinkedIn to see if they're someone you'd like to link with or follow—and then see if they're also on Twitter.

4) *Think about your contacts.* Decide if you want to upload your contacts to Twitter to see which of your contacts are also on Twitter.

5) *Keep your eyes open.* News sites frequently list Twitter handles of contributors at the bottom of articles, and LinkedIn lists Twitter handles for people in your network of connections (under "Contact info"). Go peek to see what they post about on Twitter and when they last posted. At the top of each profile page, you'll see which people, if any, who follow you also follow that person. Seeing the names of friends or people you admire can provide a credibility boost and inspire you to follow them. Similarly, people may be inspired to follow an account you follow based on the strength of your name. This phenomenon has been dubbed "social proof."

6) *Explore.* Type in a person's full name (with quotes around it, like "Oprah Winfrey") in the Twitter search field to see if they're in the Twitterverse. (If you type in Oprah's name, you'll find her handle—@Oprah—and see that she has 43 million followers.) Look for Adam Grant, the author and organizational psychologist (he's @AdamMGrant) with 602,000 followers.

tech tip Care to view the latest tweets or top tweets on your timeline? Click the star ✦ symbol at the top of your screen to toggle between the options. (I prefer latest.)

Advanced Search / Words

Advanced Search

twitter.com/search-advanced

Search

Words

All of these words

Example: what's happening • contains both "what's" and "happening"

This exact phrase

Example: happy hour • contains the exact phrase "happy hour"

Any of these words

Example: cats dogs • contains either "cats" or "dogs" (or both)

None of these words

Example: cats dogs • does not contain "cats" and does not contain "dogs"

These hashtags

Example: #throwbackThursday * contains the hashtag #ThrowbackThursday

Language
Any language

Advanced Search / Accounts

Advanced Search

twitter.com/search-advanced

(Search)

Accounts

From these accounts

Example: @Twitter • sent from @Twitter

To these accounts

Example: @Twitter • sent in reply to @Twitter

Mentioning these accounts

Example: @SFBart @Caltrain • mentions @SFBart or mentions @Caltrain

Advanced Search / Filters

Advanced Search

Search

twitter.com/search-advanced

Filters

Replies

Include replies and Original Tweets ✓

Only show replies

Links

Include Tweets with links ✓

Only show Tweets with links

Advanced Search / Engagements

Advanced Search

twitter.com/search-advanced

(Search)

Engagement

Minimum replies

Example: 280 • Tweets with at least 280 replies

Minimum Likes

Example: 280 • Tweets with at least 280 likes

Minimum Retweets

Example: 280 * Tweets with at least 280 Retweets

Advanced Search / Dates

Advanced Search

Search

twitter.com/search-advanced

Dates

From

Month ∨	Day ∨	Year ∨

To

Month ∨	Day ∨	Year ∨

Let's explore each of these methods in more detail.

Search for Topics on Twitter

You can run a search for any topic you're interested in, from diversity and innovation to AI and big data. Hashtags make it easier to search. For example, you could search the hashtag #leadership to find upcoming events, books, articles, podcasts and other sources of information on the topic of leadership.

Interested in sustainability? I am. When I saw a tweet about an innovative company named Appalachian Botanical, I retweeted it (by clicking "Quote tweet"). Here's what I said:

> Glad to know about @abcolavender, a #zerowaste company that grows lavender & raises bees on former strip mines in West Virginia & gives people a 2nd chance. By @RichieHertzberg @thehill

In my post, besides giving a genuine compliment and citing the video editor/writer and publication, I did three things:

- I included the link : https://thehill.com/changing-america/sustainability/environment/551182-how-abandoned-strip-mines-are-being-rescued-by-a/
- I added hashtags (such as #zerowaste) to make it easy for others interested in the following topics to find it—and I also added #sustainability and #innovation.

- Plus, I added a thanks ("hat tip") to the person who first posted it, my former colleague @Jeanheek.

Quick question: Let's pause for a second: Imagine it's your company that's been featured in such a positive tweet. If you handle the Twitter account, do you "like" the tweet? Share it? Yes to both! And that's what Appalachian Botanical did. It's the kind of positive PR you can't pay for.

timeless tip Hashtags are always run together as one word, with no spaces in between—like #digitalmarketing or #supportsmallbusiness.

What's Trending?

In the right-hand column on Twitter's homepage, you'll see a box with the header "What's Happening?" These are topics that are trending, either in your geographic area, nationally or in other countries. Click on "Show more" to go to a page of these trending topics. If you see an account that says "promoted" underneath it, that's a paid ad. Someone is paying to win your attention.

You don't need to make these trending topics a huge priority when planning your tweets. However, if you want to try to insert your views into the hot topics of the moment (see "newsjack" in the Glossary) or have something pertinent to say, click on the ones that are relevant to you. Warning: It can be a real time waster, a trip down the rabbit hole, as some say, to get sucked into this, so proceed with caution.

Mine Conferences

Peruse speakers' lists for people you'd like to meet. Some conferences make it easy by listing Twitter handles next to their names. At others, you may have to do a bit of digging to see if they tweet. For example, an executive communications coach spoke at a TEDx event in Mississippi. She can be found on Twitter as @RuthSherman, and she shares a wealth of tips on public speaking.

timeless tip Find and use the conference hashtag to get noticed by other attendees and organizers. Bonus: Also use the conference organizer's handle to raise your visibility.

Here's a sample tweet you can customize and use:

> Look forward to attending the [event] on [date] at [location]. Holler if you'll be there, too. [Insert the conference hashtag here as one word, such as #Techonomy22.]

Beyond simply stating that you'll be attending an event (a plain vanilla appetizer of a tweet), I recommend that you also aim to tweet something of substance—more of a main dish. For example, I suggested to a tech client who was attending the #RSASummit, a well-known, multiday cybersecurity event, to tweet a highlight from the keynote speech, which had some original insights that were relevant to him. He did, tagged the keynote speaker, and used the conference hashtag.

Not only did the speaker see his tweet, but she also made it a point—much to his surprise—to seek him out the next day at a private event to introduce herself. My client was stunned (and thrilled) that he'd made such an impression with just one tweet, but that is the mark of a good, relevant tweet.

If you're not quite sure what to say about a panel discussion, you could snap a quick photo and identify the speakers (with their Twitter handles) along with, yes, the conference hashtag. (Sticking with our food metaphor, this would be a snack.)

Speaking of conferences, here is a charming tweet I spotted while attending the Techonomy conference in Half Moon Bay, California. Someone I didn't know tweeted the following:

> @OliviaRudgard
> I'm at #Techonomy19 in Half Moon Bay today—
> come and say hello if you see me dashing around
> (British lady, short hair, big glasses, probably
> retrieving something I dropped on the floor).

After seeing that friendly tweet, I wanted to meet Olivia. The minute I saw someone at the next coffee break who fit her description (and once I checked her name badge), I introduced myself. She had made it easy. I felt like I already knew this journalist, who covered Silicon Valley for *The Telegraph* in Britain and now covers the environment.

This is the power of Twitter in business: gaining insight into a person's thinking and interests and sometimes giving you a way to know them—or know them better.

 fun fact

@NASAPersevere, NASA's Perseverance Mars rover, is tweeting from the planet Mars, thanks to @NASAJPL magic. It has 2.8 million followers.

Think About Your Contacts

Decide if you want to upload your contacts to Twitter to easily connect with them. For privacy, you may not want to. If you do upload your contacts, Twitter will show you accounts your friends are following.

In general, I'd rather find people on my own. If your contacts are active on Twitter and they tweet about topics you're interested in, you will most likely find them. If you know someone who uses Twitter, click to see who they're following, and you'll probably find a few people in common—and some new people to follow as well.

Incidentally, if you're connected to a person on LinkedIn (1st degree), click on their contact info and you will see their Twitter handle, if they've listed it (not everyone does).

timeless tip

Go to the account of someone you admire and see who they're following. Decide if you'd like to follow some of those people, too.

Keep Your Eyes Open

Be open to serendipity! After I posted an inquiry on an email list of 300 consultants, in which I asked about their experience with a new service, two wrote me back responding to my question. They seemed sharp, so I looked them up and each was on Twitter. One was a consultant with her own environmental podcast, and she immediately gained a new follower—me.

You don't have to meet in person to forge a connection. Sometimes you fall in love a little thanks to a person's tweets, and that person may very well "like" your tweets in turn and share them with the world.

One of my favorite philosophies is this one, posted by an independent film producer:

> @TedHope
> You have to find a way to conspire with people you have yet to meet.

Ted and I have yet to meet, but I'm already a fan. If and when you do connect with a person, whether online or in the flesh, they can become part of your extended community and you can be part of theirs.

Entrepreneur Gefen Skolnick (@chiefgayofficer) has had excellent luck reaching out to people on Twitter who inspire her and advises others to do the same. Likewise, Minal Hasan, a Silicon Valley venture capitalist who tweets under @Minal_Hasan, posted this advice:

> Ladies, shoot your shot. Hit up people's DMs for opportunities. Trust me, the men are, and you are often more qualified. Nothing to lose!

By "hit up people's DMs" she's suggesting people send direct messages (see Chapter 5 and the Glossary).

Explore

Curiosity can be well rewarded on Twitter. Headed on a business trip to Nashville for the first time? Look up music venues and museum handles in your destination. Follow a few, or create a list (see Chapter 5).

Ever typed in your name to see what comes up? I follow several people on Twitter who have a similar last name to mine but aren't related. One is a witty, food-obsessed divorce lawyer in New York; another is an LA-based producer, streamer and activist for disabled people. I started following them just for fun, but following each and interacting with them has broadened my horizons (Hi, @tkretchmar and

@dreamwisp). Sometimes I retweet them and sometimes they retweet me, which spreads my name beyond my usual circles.

Often, someone you follow will tweet something of note that also catches your interest. That's how I came across the following post talking about Twitter from Rabbi Danya Ruttenberg:

> @TheRaDR
> One of the best things about this platform is how much you can learn from so many experiences and perspectives. For free. If you've never done an audit of your follows & thought about whose voices you're hearing & whose not, do it.

As you explore, you'll see that many people tweet about more than their business life. You'll find oodles of people talking about their kids, their pets and more. The topics you tweet about are up to you. What's the balance that is right for you? As a somewhat private person, I don't talk about my life much, but I enjoy sharing the occasional post about books (and the hashtag #littlefreelibraries), movies or music.

For more inspiration and ideas, peruse the most recent tweets of people you admire. Here are a few accounts of well-known people who tweet frequently:

@AriannaHuff
@MelindaGates
@AvaDuVernay

@levie (CEO of Box, a tech company)
@BillGates
@StephenKing

Unlikely Allies, Drawing Audiences

True confession: Stephen King's hugely popular horror novels are too scary for my tastes, but I find his tweets to be charming, especially when he interacts with other people. As an example, a famed movie critic remarked in December 2019 about the premiere of the movie remake *Little Women* and noted that the acclaimed movie was not drawing in enough male moviegoers:

> @JanetMaslin
> The Little Women problem with men is very real. I don't say that lightly and am very alarmed. In the past day have been told by 3 male friends who usually trust me that they either refuse to see it or probably won't have time. Despite my saying it's tied for #1 of 2019.

More than 6,000 people liked her tweet, and 1,300 commented, including a certain author:

> @StephenKing
> Based on your recommendation, I will watch it even though I'm guessing nothing gets blown up.

That exchange inspired King to go see the movie. Guess who else it inspired? Me, and probably thousands. It's the kind of positive buzz that producers, authors and other creators dream of.

The Lowdown on Building Your Following

Unless you're a major celebrity who already attracts attention from fans, the three main ways to grow one's following boil down to a simple recipe:

- Be interesting. Tweet observations, comments and experiences that people are interested in. This works well for tech people, venture capitalists and investors.
- Be human. Interact with people; don't just automate your tweets to go out at scheduled times. Acknowledge people's comments. Retweet when it makes sense.
- Be consistent. You pick the topics and timetable that are right for you. Some sales and marketing people tweet three to five times a day or more.

Best Practices to Build Your Following

Below are additional ideas to build your following, online and in person. Be open to opportunities and serendipity. If you meet interesting people, search for information about them online and see if you have something in common.

- **Act locally.** One of the best ways to build your following is to network locally with people where you have a natural connection and then stay in touch via Twitter.

For example, you can meet people in your community at a professional meetup and then support them online by sharing relevant tweets of theirs that resonate with you. Then, after you get to know them, you can ask them to do the same for you. I interact with two people on my Twitter feed regularly: Dennis Shiao (@Dshiao) and Rich Schwerin (@greencognito). In fact, I introduced them years ago when they were organizing meetups for bloggers and other content creators in the heart of Silicon Valley, and they joined forces. Both promote @Content_Meetup in newspaper ads, in emails, on LinkedIn and, of course, on Twitter. They regularly attracted more than a dozen people to their in-person meetings before the COVID-19 pandemic hit in spring 2020; then they went virtual and began holding weekly online meetings for a global audience.

- **Professors, lawyers and VCs, oh my.** People in certain professions tend to use Twitter, and if you mention a frequent Twitter user, they're likely to retweet or at least "like" your tweet. That can grow your following. If you want to post about any academic or research studies of the past five years, for example, search to see if the professor and publication use Twitter and then tag them. The same goes for friendly journalists, including @karaswisher and @DanRather, and certain companies and celebrities, such as @hootsuite and @netflix, @MarkHamill (actor Mark Hamill, 5 million followers) or

@GeorgeTakei (actor and activist George Takei, 3.3 million followers).

- **Be generous; build goodwill.** When you share someone else's tweet, you're more likely to get a follow or get someone to amplify your tweets in turn. Amplify a message. Reply to others. Congratulate a colleague on their new podcast. Book publicist Tina LoSasso (@TinaLoSasso) has a circle of colleagues who share one another's works, which can help create new leads for everyone. Building a following can be a difficult, painstaking task; by following people who are willing to follow you back, and by sharing other people's tweets who then reciprocate by sharing yours, you are helping to create a community of mutual support, where everybody wins.

- **Share your coworkers' messages** when they're on brand, and ask them to do the same for you. If you're a solopreneur, look for a friend in an adjacent or related industry. (For example, if you're an executive coach in the Midwest, you could share wisdom from a coaching friend in the Southwest.)

- **Share useful tips.** Here's a type of tip that other knowledge workers might find insightful. A professional search firm called Westwood & Wilshire shared the following on a Thursday:

@westwoodwilshir

Feeling the weekday slump? Our team recently had the opportunity to hear productivity expert @mnthomas discuss methods to increase productivity via attn management. "Focus and attention are skills like any other: If you don't use them, you lose them." #ThursdayThoughts

- **Cultivate community, whether it's with business owners, tech marketers or tea connoisseurs.** Look for topics that interest you and consider responding. If you tweet on these topics, use relevant hashtags such as #entrepreneurs, #SMB, #tech or #tea.

The tweet below generated several hundred responses, and the person who asked the question, Harley Finkelstein, president of Shopify, responded to nearly all.

@harleyf

Business & entrepreneur Twitter: I'm curious, what's the best habit you've developed to take care of your mental health while building a business?

If a person with a big following shares your tweet, you will of course reach many more people than you normally would. As examples, journalist and professor Sree Sreenivasan (@sree) posts regularly about current events and generously mentions others. And tech marketing guru and pundit Scott Galloway (@profgalloway) tweets often (about his talks, podcasts and interviews, as well as about his dogs and his family), and he frequently retweets others to his 441,000 followers.

Whether you're a tea aficionado or simply admire acts of generosity, be on the lookout for others who share your passion and could become part of your community. For example, here's a witty tweet by an Irish artist that might strike your fancy:

> @killersundymann
> I just wanted a cup of tea but then I asked if anyone else wanted tea and now I work in catering.

Speaking of tea, Friday Afternoon Tea (@FridayTea), a popular Seattle hangout, retweeted a compliment when a new customer (@fallentako) mentioned receiving a package from them and "geeking out over the random themed teas I got." The shop also answered a question from the customer with a whimsical GIF, delighting that person.

Ask yourself: If it's your business, will you take the time to be as thoughtful? It could win you a lifetime customer—or many more.

Take a tip from advocacy groups and make it super-easy for people to share your messages.

Many advocacy groups and socially minded business endeavors make big splashes online because they know how to energize their troops. They create social media toolkits for allies to share their messages. To increase the number of people who see your tweets, follow the example of @NewMediaVenture and write sample messages for colleagues, with hashtags, and ask them to share these messages on a certain day. Some recipients may do nothing, but others will copy and paste your message exactly as is. A few enterprising people will even customize it. Thank them!

timeless tip

- **Follow Twitter's recommendations.** When Twitter recommends people to follow, click on their profile and glance at their bio. Look interesting? Follow them. (If they haven't tweeted in a long time, of course, don't bother.) Twitter also now heavily promotes topics, some of which will show up in the middle of your newsfeed or on the margins. Some will also likely be of interest to you. There's also an option to mark a topic as "not interested," so it doesn't keep showing up.

- **Follow back.** One key way to widen your network is to "follow back"—follow people who follow you. Peruse their bio and see if it's a good fit. If they have poor grammar, very few followers or a string of numbers after their name, they could be a bot. In that case, don't follow back. (As noted earlier, you can see why it's useful to have a decent Twitter bio, so people don't dismiss you upfront.)

In the next chapter, we'll look at how to tweet efficiently. But before we move on, take a look back and see whether you've gone after the easiest, low-hanging fruit. In other words, have you:

- Listed a URL in your Twitter bio pointing to your website, company page or LinkedIn profile so that people who are interested can find out more?
- Uploaded a header image that's right for your personality, your brand or your latest campaign, whether that's for a new product or book?
- Looked for people who share your interests so you can follow one another?
- Repeated my mantra that retweeting is good karma and better than a like?

timeless tip

On the number of followers:
When you're starting out, you'll follow more people than follow you; don't stress. Eventually you might aim to follow roughly as many accounts as the number following you or maybe 100 more than follow you.

5
So Many Tweets, So Little Time

You have ideas on what you'd like to tweet about and which types of conversations you'd like to follow on Twitter. The trick now is to accomplish your goals without getting sucked in for hours and hours. It's not easy, but here are some strategies to help you. Yes, there are scheduling tools available, but first skim these tips.

How to Save Time on Twitter

First, have a basic strategy. If you are highly disciplined, set a timer and only hop on Twitter for 10 minutes. Here's what you could do during that time:

Click on Notifications (the bell symbol in the left-hand menu) to see who, if anyone, has mentioned you. If someone has, decide if you want to respond. Ask yourself, do they look legit? Are they from a group or company you know? Do they have a decent number of followers (say, more than 20)? What have they tweeted about lately? If they're only tweeting about things that don't interest you, or if their Twitter handle looks computer-generated and they have no followers, they're not worth your time. Under Notifications, you can also see if there are any interesting topics that catch your interest.

Decide if you are going to send out a tweet or two now or later via a scheduling tool (more about that in a minute).

Look at your editorial calendar of upcoming events for inspiration, such as the launch of a new product or topics to talk about on certain days with popular hashtags such as #WednesdayWisdom, #ThrowbackThursday or #SmallBusinessSaturday.

good karma
retweet! don't just like

In a Hurry? 3 Things You Can Do Now

In a rush? It doesn't take much time to make an impression, get informed or create good karma.

Peruse your newsfeed. Look for something that captures your interest and decide which of these three things you'll do. All of them can be done lickety-split, but they're listed in order of their time commitment—from shortest to longest.

1) **Like:** Like a tweet but not sure what to say about it? Or perhaps you'd first like to read an article it links to. Hit the heart-shaped "Like" button and consider coming back to it another time. (That only took half a second!)

2) **Retweet:** Find a tweet that resonates with you? Share it with others. Retweet it by clicking the retweet button underneath (the double arrow square). Retweeting is

good karma! Someone might do it for you, too.

3) **Quote Tweet:** If you have more time and the tweet inspires a thought of your own, click the retweet button and select "quote tweet." Then post your thoughts. It could be as short as, "Worth a read." Congrats. You may have just made someone's day. And you're increasing your odds of good karma.

Time-Saving Strategies for Branding

Here's a time-saving strategy I recommended for a busy marketing team at a B2B company to raise awareness of their product among potential customers:

- **Use Twitter to meet your overall marketing/personal branding goals.** In other words, don't think of Twitter as a separate marketing goal. Instead, use Twitter to accomplish your goals!

- **Tweet strategically.** Use your tweets to promote and "amplify" issues and topics that matter to you, including articles, books, webinars and podcasts.

- **Share (retweet) others' info when relevant.** Some say you should retweet at a 3:1 ratio, meaning retweeting others' material three times for every one tweet of your own. You could even try a 4:1 ratio.

- **Focus on quality, not quantity.** Don't worry about having a huge following. Aim instead for a targeted group of followers who are interested in what you offer. Nearly 96 percent of Twitter users have fewer than 500 followers.

Learn to Love Lists

Lists are challenging to describe, but they're somewhat of a cool, little-known feature. They're curated lists of topics and accounts, such as people who attended a certain conference, and you can follow a list to keep up with people you're interested in. You can subscribe to a list or just peruse a list rather than follow each of the accounts mentioned. Imagine it's a list with 100 "members" on it. You can view it two main ways: by the latest tweets from that group, which will show you who's most active now, or by clicking through to glance at each member's profile (some won't have tweeted in ages).

To see lists, go to your profile page and click on "Lists" in the menu on the left-hand side. Twitter will offer you suggestions for lists you might like to follow. If you'd like to see my lists, check out my profile (@LKhere), click on the three parallel dots at the top of the header image and then select "View Lists." You can see two types: lists I'm on—these are lists others have put me on (including Awesome Tweeters)—and public lists I've created, such as a popular one for scientists called Evol Biology + Science (I set it up to track a family member's postdoctoral work in biology). You won't see my private lists, however, as they're private!

One entrepreneur swears by her private lists as handy reference tools, including a list with 650 women business leaders she's cultivating as prospective clients and good people to know. Instead of following each of their 650 individual accounts, which would be time-consuming and overwhelming, she can browse and keep up with their news by periodically checking her list. (In so doing, she's also keeping the number of people she's following down.)

To see some intriguing lists in the startup world, go to the profiles of some entrepreneurs who are active Twitter users and click to see what lists they subscribe to. If you look up entrepreneur Gefen Skolnick (@chiefgayofficer), for example, here's what you'll find. Click on the three dots to view the lists Skolnick subscribes to and the "lists they're on" (the latter includes lists called Startup Advice, Female Founders + CEOs and Twitter Must Follows). If the topics interest you, then you too can follow those lists. You can also, as mentioned, check for lists on others' profiles or follow any of Twitter's suggestions.

fun fact

If you subscribe to another person's public list, it will then show up and be accessible via your profile. Look for your list tab.

A Word About Scheduling Tools

Many busy people like to use social media scheduling tools, such as TweetDeck (acquired by Twitter), Buffer, Hootsuite, SocialFlow or Sprout Social. With these tools, you can plan your social media posts in advance and queue them up to go out at specific times. Some folks even hire virtual assistants or low-level interns to manage their social media for them.

This may sound like heresy, but I find the tools to be fairly similar. If you do decide to use a tool, pick the one that works for your budget. I sometimes use Hootsuite.

However, bear in mind that you can't just put your tweets on autopilot and forget about them. If world or local news intervenes or tragedy strikes, you'll want to put your automated social media on hold to make sure the messages are still relevant and not tone-deaf.

Remember, too, that the true value in Twitter is interacting in real time in your authentic voice. If you merely line up your tweets to go out automatically, that's just an old-style broadcast system. And people will know it, as the bottom of the tweet shows how it was sent (on the web, via a phone or through a scheduling tool).

Be real: If you decide to rely on Twitter scheduling tools, such as Buffer, also make time for some "live" and in-the-moment tweets. That way, you can respond to messages that come in, so you don't come across as canned. If you have someone else managing your social media, be sure to look at it periodically. Is it reflecting the real you? Does it sound like the professional you? If not, adjust it. Or, as the tech crowd says, pivot!

good karma
retweet! don't just like

timeless tip

If someone you respect says something highly positive about you or your company, retweet it! Don't just hit "like." Share their comment with your following. It's good karma, and a retweet reaches more people than a like.

Another good rule of thumb: Be gentle with yourself. Some days, such as the ones before a webinar, may result in a lot of social media activity. Other days, not as much.

Share Info (and Save Time): Tweet It or DM It

See a hot new article from *The Information* or *Harvard Business Review* that you want to share with a colleague? Or an intriguing video clip? Tweet it and tag them (assuming they use Twitter, too. If not, give them a copy of this book!) It's much faster and more efficient than writing an email or sending a text. Not only will they see it, but other people who are interested in the same topic are likely to see it, too.

If you don't want everyone in your feed to see it, you can send it via DM (direct message). Usually someone needs to follow you for you to be able to DM them, and many customer service accounts, such as those run by the major airlines, ask people to follow them so that they can DM the customers and not share sensitive information openly.

Some users have "open" DMs, meaning anyone can

message them. I don't recommend it. You're likely to attract unwanted interest from strangers. Occasionally you'll come across people who say "no DMs" in their Twitter bios, as they find it annoying.

DMs can be very useful with those you know and trust. My brother, a politically minded friend and I DM frequently to share info—it's our private back channel among the three of us when we see something of interest, and it's faster than texting.

Here's how to DM: Log in and look for the envelope icon. Click on it and search for the Twitter handle of the person you want to DM and type a short message; then click the arrow next to the text box to send it. To forward a tweet by DM, click on the Share button underneath the tweet (the one with the upward-pointing arrow, on the right), then choose "Send via Direct Message."

Direct Messages

Direct Messages

Home	Search	Spaces	Notifications	Direct Messages

This is a direct message - it's like a private text

Monitoring the Monitoring Tools

Let's talk about tools. Some people swear by them as time-savers. Let's also talk about results. Many marketing and businesspeople want to know the numbers behind any activity—what's the measurement? What will get measured? What's the return on investment? Is it worth it?

But let's get real. If you've just launched a Twitter account and only tweeted a few times, your numbers will be quite low. Think of it this way: If you were just learning how to swim, you would not, I hope, be racing to learn how judges in international competitions rate divers. Learn to swim first, and then maybe think about diving. Get your feet wet, learn the basics of tweeting and then start looking at analytics in 30 or 60 days.

tech tip

What if the person complaining is a paying customer? If you're using Twitter to interact with customers, ask them to follow your account so that you can DM them to get more information, if needed. In general, you don't have the ability to contact people privately (via DM) unless they follow your account. Browse Twitter and you'll see airline companies, hotels and other service providers interacting with customers. To see Twitter itself in action, follow @TwitterSupport and check the "replies' tab.

Indeed, Twitter currently offers free extensive analytics per post that cover the past 18 months or so on its website. Log in to twitter.com, and in the left-hand menu click on "More" and then "Analytics." Or go directly to **analytics.twitter.com.** You can look at your total number of tweets, tweet impressions, profile visits, mentions and followers versus the previous 28-day summary, plus your monthly top tweet (the one with the most impressions), top mention (most engagements), top follower (most followers) and top media tweet (most impressions for a post with a photo or video). Seek even more reach? Click on "go to ads" at the upper right and consider an ad campaign.

For stats while you're on the go, look under one of your tweets on the app, and then click on the image of a line graph. You'll see analytics, including impressions, total engagements, detail expands, likes, profile clicks, retweets and replies. Once you've built up some momentum, you'll see that tweets that initially garner just a few likes or retweets may accrue umpteen times more impressions, as many more people view (or "lurk") on social media than retweet or comment. When I tweeted about an upcoming book-author talk, the tweet got 17 likes, 1 retweet, 2 responses—and an impressive 13,900 impressions, a higher reach than one might guess. When I quoted a journalist on the topic of diversity, it received 29 likes, 12 retweets—and 15,300 impressions.

Huge engagement is not my priority; engagement with the right people is.

The best metrics are when you engage the people you want to reach. Maybe they like your post and will check out your product. Maybe they sign up to buy tickets to your event. Maybe they bookmark your TED Talk and tell five friends, who tell five of their friends, and you then get invited to make paid speeches at companies you admire.

The ideas you post can add value to others and increase their opinion of your work, even if you're already well known. Here are Twitter metrics that tech analyst Benedict Evans, @benedictevans, who has 347,000 followers, shared about one month after he posted a link to his latest annual presentation on tech trends. It showed the tweet received 1 million impressions, 21,951 link clicks, 2,845 likes, 1,018 retweets, 87 replies including many thanks, 3,180 profile visits and 28 new followers.

For marketing departments and people highly interested in data, there are many tools available to help you measure your reach on Twitter. For example, with Sprout Social, a tool for managing a team of people tweeting or for managing multiple social media accounts, you can delve into your or your team's posts with the "highest engagement," meaning the tweets that are the most popular with people on Twitter.

According to Sprout, "If engagement is your goal, sorting by the most engaged posts will help you find similarities among these posts so you can determine which elements appeal most to people and optimize your future content." They say their technology analyzes patterns and can let you know the optimal times to post your content for the highest engagement.

Be aware that some of the worst and nastiest social media content has the highest engagement, as has been well reported by researchers and the media.

There are tons of analytics tools available. Sometimes the tool you pick may come down to your budget or what your client uses. To see what tools others are using, just click on the time they tweeted. At the bottom of the tweet you may see Twitter Web App or Twitter for iPhone or Android (meaning they were tweeted "live" from those platforms), or Hootsuite, Buffer, Sprout and so forth.

There are many tools on the market, from free (for basic plans) to six figures. Hootsuite and Buffer both have free versions. Keyhole, for about $50 per month and up, provides data on social listening, account analytics, influencer management and quick trends; Sprinklr, used by enterprise companies, costs in the range of $100,000 a year.

The Opposite of Attracting Followers: When to Block or Mute

To save valuable time, remember not to engage with trolls or other abusive people. You most likely won't change their minds, so why waste precious time and energy?

In general, there may be times when you'd rather not add a certain follower to your community, even if they'd boost your numbers. If you find a person's Twitter account objectionable, you can block it from your view. If they're a friend or relative (someone where it might be awkward if you never see their content), you can simply "mute" their activity and not see their tweets as often. If the content is highly inappropriate, you can report it to Twitter.

In conclusion, you'll need to seek your own best balance between your urge to be on Twitter versus the amount of time you'd like to spend on it, and who you want to hear from and interact with.

Down the line your interests may change, and that's fine, too.

Here's to you, amplifying your brand, in the ways that work best for you.

Glossary

Readers, thank you in advance for skimming the glossary. Also see **help.twitter.com**. Please reach out and say hi to me on Twitter (I'm at @LKhere) or via my website: **upwithsocial. com/book**

Advanced search: A free tool on the Twitter website and app to peruse tweets.

Bio: See *Twitter bio.*

Blue checkmark: See *Verified.*

Bookmarks: Click on the upward arrow beneath a tweet and you'll have the opportunity to "Bookmark" or save a tweet. Sometimes people use "Like" as a bookmark. Either way, you can return to it another time and decide if you want to learn more about it by, say, reading a linked article or retweeting it.

Community: A new feature Twitter is rolling out to help creators and certain groups find each other, such as Black makeup artists. They are like private groups for people to find fellowship.

Creator: A user who creates something to sell, such as videos, blog posts, podcasts, animation or real-world goods. Twitter is increasingly adding features to appeal to this growing group.

CTA: Call to action. The thing marketers want people to do once they've seen a tweet or some other marketing message. Buy, sign up, tell a friend.

DM: Short for direct message, this is a way to communicate privately with other Twitter users. Usually, someone has to be following your account for you to send them a DM, although "DMs open" means a person will accept DMs from anyone, not just from the people they are following. Be aware that sometimes Twitter users who allow open DMs get harassed by trolls.

Direct message: See *DM*.

Downvote: The ability to vote down another person's comment, if, for example, you don't think it adds to the discourse. Look for a downward arrow icon under replies.

Drafts: A function on your phone to save a tweet in progress. Look for the quill-like icon to find it again. It can be hard to find sometimes!

Engagement: When people click, share or like your posts. These actions are a measure of interest. The higher, the better—unless they're a troll.

Feed: Short for newsfeed; also known as the timeline. The place where all the tweets flow in from the accounts you're following. By default, it sorts tweets by "top" (most popular, according to Twitter's algorithms), or you can change it to "latest," which I vastly prefer. The newsfeed is on the homepage; go to an account's profile page to view tweets from that account.

Handles: Twitter usernames, such as @LKhere.

Hashtags: Topics of interest, conference names, movies and books, and more—all compressed into one word or phrase, beginning with a hashtag (e.g., #BlackLivesMatter or #blackgamers). They help make topics easily searchable for others interested in the topic. Sometimes people try to hijack a hashtag and use it to promote an opposing point of view.

Hat tip: Think of a metaphorical tip of the hat, as in thanking a person for pointing out news of interest.

Header image: The big horizontal image at the top of your Twitter profile.

Influencer: A person building a platform to be used by brands for marketing purposes and to make money. Sometimes used for people with big audiences in your area of interest whose opinion holds sway.

Latest: One of the two main ways to view your Twitter news-feed (and other social media). Latest shows the most recent tweets for the accounts a person follows. There's also Top, which shows the most popular tweets as determined by an algorithm (I prefer Latest).

Like: A way to show your approval or interest in a tweet. Click on the heart-shaped button below the tweet. Your "likes" are like personal bookmarks for you to refer back to. Look for them under your "Tweets & Replies" tab. Remember that if you have a public account, your likes are public, too. (Note: Retweets are a more valuable way to show appreciation.)

List: A robust way to create groups of accounts you'd like to follow without having to follow each one individually. You can create your own lists or subscribe to someone else's, and they will show up on your profile's Lists page for handy reference. Lists can be public or private.

Live tweets: When an event posts tweets as it's happening. If you are asked to do this or want to do this, the trick is to plan as much as possible in advance (for example, have a list of Twitter handles for the speakers, get photos ready to upload and have prewritten tweets to post or tweak at the right time). Live tweeting is a skill, and we applaud those who do it well.

Lurk: A person who watches what's going on but doesn't like, tweet or comment. Most people, in fact, do this. Not the same intent as stalking, although your teenager may disagree.

mDAU: Monetizable daily active users. Twitter's key metric for people, organizations and other accounts who access it and see ads and other paid products.

Monetization: Making money from your social media account. You almost always need a sizable audience. See also *Super Follow.*

Newsfeed: See *Feed.* Also *Timeline.*

Newsjack: A portmanteau of "news" and "hijack." Taking the day's news and trying to make your content relevant in some way, usually in hopes of boosting engagement.

Newsletter: Twitter has purchased a newsletter company called Revue. It provides a newsletter option for those who wish to correspond with their audiences.

Organic: Free. Opposite of a paid ad, boost or tweet.

Private: A way to control who sees an account. You can only view a private account if the person who runs it accepts your request. Most accounts are public.

Profile: This is your page showing your tweets and the tweets you've liked. I think of it as one level down from the news-feed. You can toggle back and forth between the two views. The latest tweets from others show up in your newsfeed; your past tweets are shown on your profile.

Profile pic: The image that appears on your profile page and next to your tweets and replies; generally, friendly headshots are best.

Promote: This nice verb has been hijacked. It's now synon-ymous with paying to boost visibility (that is, buying an ad). Sometimes you'll see a "promoted" tweet in your newsfeed—meaning they paid to be there. Do you like the ad? Does it resonate? Sometimes it does! If you promote a tweet, you'll want it to resonate.

Quote tweet: When you add a comment to a retweet, which shows up on top of the original tweet.

Ratioed: When someone posts a remark on Twitter, usually political in nature, and then receives many more replies than likes or retweets. Usually, this means many people disagree with the comment.

Replies: Twitter has begun offering options for Twitter ac-count holders to select who can respond (for example, everyone or simply people you mention and "people you follow"). Twitter also lets people hide replies. The goal is more user control and less abuse.

Retweet: A valuable way to show appreciation for someone else's tweet. Click on the circular arrow underneath a tweet to share it with everyone in your feed. It's good karma!

Share: The act of sharing a tweet with your followers. A retweet is a share. Theoretically all your followers could see it (although they won't all be online at the time).

Social listening: Listening to your markets, competitors, prospects and customers by viewing the topics they tweet about and talk about.

Social selling: Selling via having an active social media presence in which you engage with people.

Spaces: Social audio, popularized by the app known as Clubhouse. You can have conversations with people and participate in or host live conversations. Twitter has also added the option to record these conversations for later playback.

Subtweet: When someone tweets about another person (usually a famous or prominent one) without tagging them or saying their name.

Super Follow: A new feature for creators to accept money tips from supportive fans and followers, a concept popularized by Patreon, the crowdfunding site for creators.

Tag: Mentioning someone's handle in a tweet, such as @TwitterMktg for Twitter Marketing. Can be a smart way to get noticed and share good vibes.

Thread: Posting a series of tweets when you have a lot to say. You create the series by: 1) replying to your own tweet, or 2) using Twitter's built-in tool (see the + sign). Sometimes signified by the emoji of a spool of thread.

Timeline: Another term for the newsfeed, where you can view the tweets from people you follow.

Tips: The ability to accept payment from users. Must have a Twitter for Professionals account.

TLDR: Too long, didn't read

Top: One of the two main ways to view your Twitter newsfeed. Top goes by the most popular, according to algorithms. I prefer Latest, which shows the most recent tweets for the accounts I follow.

Troll: Mean, obnoxious people on social media, usually trying to hide their identity. Whenever possible, do not engage. They're not worth your time.

Tweet: A post on Twitter. Originally you had only 140 characters. Now you have 280.

Twitter: The microblogging platform launched in 2006. Creative genius Lin-Manuel Miranda has called it "an audience up in my pocket." Some call it the bird app.

Twitter bio: Describe yourself and your interests—you have 160 characters. See Chapter 2.

Twitter Blue: A new program Twitter has launched for active users to pay a monthly subscription fee for added features and perks, such as the opportunity to bookmark saved content or undo a tweet before it goes live.

Twitter for Professionals: A new service Twitter is rolling out, mainly for creators and brands to grow their audiences and make money. Provides access to new ad formats.

Username: Another term for handle. You have 15 characters!

Verified: The blue check (actually a white check on a blue background) on a person's profile signifying verification has become a status symbol, meaning that Twitter has verified the identity of the person or brand so that they are who they say they are, and not an impostor. Twitter promises to make this process more accessible to more people.

Viral, as in going viral: Not generally a useful or worthy goal. Tweets and other social media posts "go viral" when they become extremely popular, usually for silly, odd or scandalous reasons.

Web3: Good question! It could be the next iteration of the Web. We'll see.

Acknowledgments

Thank you very much to everyone who has inspired me to write this book. As Tina LoSasso says, publishing a book is like giving birth to an elephant.

To my 20something kid who opens my eyes all the time to new things, especially pathos, animation, manga and much more, and to family, particularly my sibs Michael and Julie, and many friends and squad members!

To illustrator Michele Grey, and big thanks to Rosemary Brisco, who first introduced me to Michele.

To book editor Marla Markman and her extended team, including Kelly Cleary and Wyn Hilty, and Paul Freiberger, who introduced me to Marla.

To my English teachers, particularly Jeannine Antypas.

To the secretary whose name I don't know who worked for my late Papa Paul, decades ago in Milwaukee and told me that someday I'd write a book.

To you for skimming, reading or perusing.

About the Author

Laurie Kretchmar is a communications strategist and former business journalist (*FORTUNE, The Wall Street Journal* and founding editor in chief of Women.com Networks). She advises consultants, marketing professionals and executives on how to establish and amplify their brands. A hands-on coach, Laurie is known for her detective skills, insights, passion for connecting people and, of course, her love of the so-called "bird app." Via her boutique consulting agencies, Up with Social and Content Marketing Place, Laurie guides thought leadership and social media for executives at companies including Applied Materials, Cisco, Dell, Malwarebytes, Samsung, SoFi and VISA. She advises social enterprise and nonprofit leaders. Laurie also speaks and acts as a moderator on webinars and at conferences worldwide. A graduate of Dartmouth College, Laurie lives in the San Francisco Bay Area.

Grow and amplify your social media marketing and thought leadership. Go to:

upwithsocial.com

On Twitter, follow: @LKhere

Index

Index

Index

Index

9 798986 206806